HISTORIC

COMMUNITIES

Pioneer Projects

Bobbie Kalman

Photographs by Marc Crabtree
Illustrations by Barbara Bedell

 Crabtree Publishing Company

HISTORIC
COMMUNITIES

Created by Bobbie Kalman

For Amanda Vernal with love

Editor-in-Chief
Bobbie Kalman

Writing team
Bobbie Kalman
Niki Walker
Greg Nickles
Hannelore Sotzek
Lynda Hale

Managing editor
Lynda Hale

Editors
Niki Walker
Greg Nickles
Petrina Gentile
Hannelore Sotzek

Computer design
Lynda Hale

Printer
Worzalla Publishing Company

Special thanks to
Peta-Gay Ramos (on cover), Krista Braniff,
Allison Vernal, Amanda Vernal, Kevin Spicer,
Philip Han, Marc Crabtree, Barbara Bedell,
Diana Boisvert, Mary George, Marnie Spicer,
Connie Warner, Genessee Country Museum,
Elmlea Junior School, St. Catharines Historical
Museum, Fort George National Historic Park,
Jordan Historical Museum of the Twenty

Illustrations and photographs
All illustrations by Barbara Bedell
All photographs were taken by Marc Crabtree
   except the following:
Bobbie Kalman: pages 3 (background),
   23 (top left), 28
David Schimpky: pages 5 (bottom left), 21

Separations and film
Dot 'n Line Image Inc.

Crabtree Publishing Company

350 Fifth Avenue
Suite 3308
New York
N.Y. 10118

360 York Road, RR 4
Niagara-on-the-Lake
Ontario, Canada
L0S 1J0

73 Lime Walk
Headington
Oxford OX3 7AD
United Kingdom

Cataloging in Publication Data
Bobbie Kalman
   Pioneer projects

(Historic communities series)
Includes index.
ISBN 0-86505-437-1 (library bound) ISBN 0-86505-467-3 (pbk.)
This book presents instructions for handicrafts and activities
in the spirit of the pioneers, including decoupage, hooked rugs,
cornhusk dolls, and making a Jacob's Ladder.

1. Frontier and pioneer life—North America—Study and
teaching—Activity programs. 2. North America—Social life and
customs—19th century—Study and teaching—Activity programs.
I. Title. II. Series: Kalman, Bobbie. Historic communities.

E179.5.K36 1997   j745.5'0973   LC 96-29943
                                                              CIP

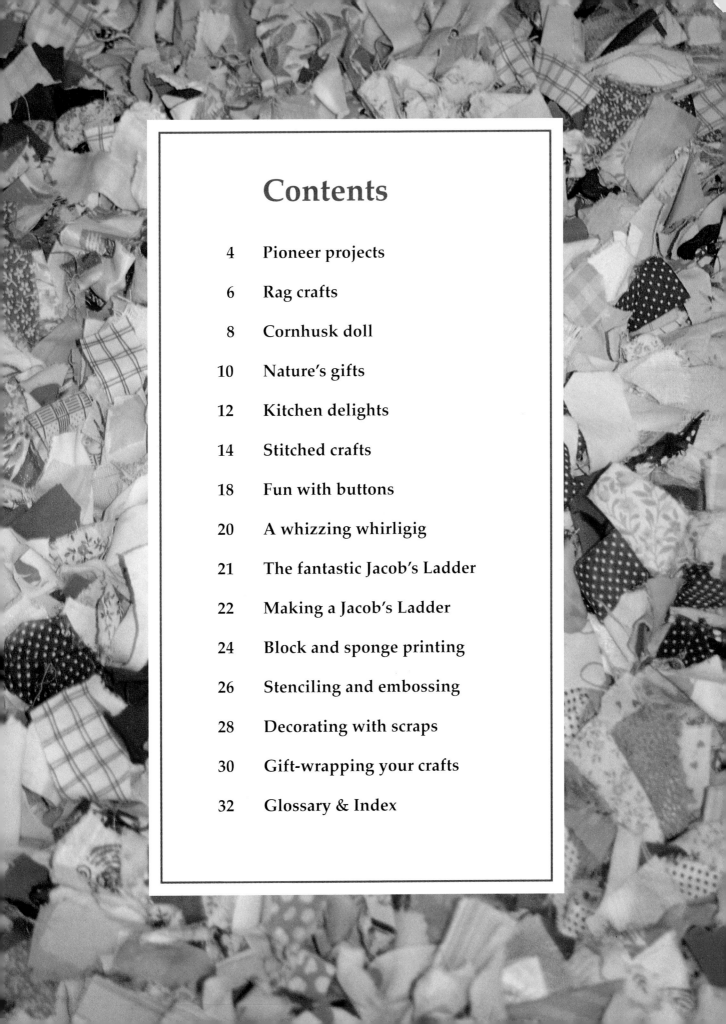

Contents

Pioneer projects

The pioneers could not afford to throw away anything, no matter how worn out it became. Clothing and bedding that could no longer be passed down to other people were ripped into strips and used to make quilts or rag rugs. Buttons were cut off and saved to be used later. Old sweaters were unraveled, and the yarn was used for mending clothes or knitting bed covers. Candle ends were saved and melted down to make new candles. The pioneers also used things that grew in their area, such as fruits, vegetables, leaves, and berries, to create toys, treats, and gifts.

Many of the pioneer-style crafts in this book can be made with things you find in your home or around the neighborhood. When you are working on these projects, remember that the pioneers had to reuse and recycle everything. In order to reduce garbage and other pollution, we must do the same today. So, think like a pioneer and have fun trying these crafts! Make sure an adult is always nearby to help you with knives, cooking, paints, and any difficult steps.

Dried apple peels can be placed at the bottom of a gift basket. They smell wonderful!

You can make a pot rest and pin cushion with a few scraps of cloth and some simple stitches.

Pioneer children played with homemade toys such as these cornhusk dolls.

No pioneer cat would have worn this bonnet, but Snoozer loves to dress up.

Rag crafts

The pioneers did not have wall-to-wall carpeting in their homes. They had either wooden or dirt floors, which were covered with rag rugs. Pioneers tore worn-out clothing and bedding into strips and then braided these scraps together or hooked them onto a backing to make rugs. Burlap bags, which were used to package and ship goods, were cut apart and used as sturdy backings for the hooked rugs.

Not only were rag rugs useful and inexpensive to make, but they also added color to the pioneer home. You can hook or braid a small rag rug to brighten your own home.

Braided rug

You need:
- 3 long strips of fabric about 1 inch (2.5 cm) wide
- 2 safety pins
- needle and thread

1. Pin together the three strips of fabric at one end.
2. Ask a friend to hold the end for you or shut it in a drawer, leaving the strips hanging free.
3. Braid the three strips together as tightly as you can, and when you come to the end, secure it with a safety pin.

4. Sew the braid where it is pinned at each end, so it will not unravel.
5. Tightly curl in one end of the braid and secure it with a stitch. Continue winding the braid around itself.
6. On one side only, stitch the coil every inch (2.5 cm) along the way until you reach the end.

Hooked rug

You need:
- piece of burlap
- strips of cotton fabric, about $^1/_2$ inch (1 cm) wide and 6 inches (15 cm) long
- crochet hook or rug-hooking tool

1. Hold a strip of fabric against the underside of the burlap.
2. Push down the hook through a hole in the burlap.
3. Hook the fabric strip and gently pull it through the burlap until it makes a loop on the top side of the burlap.
4. Remove the hook from the loop.
5. Skip over a hole on the burlap and pull up another loop of fabric.
6. When you have finished one rag strip, start hooking a new one.

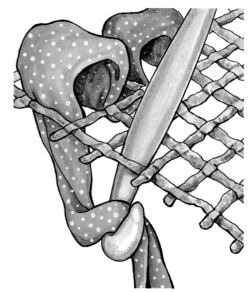

A small braided rug can be used as a pot rest or worn as an earring!

You can put your hooked rug on the floor, hang it on a wall, or make a pillow cover with it.

Cornhusk doll

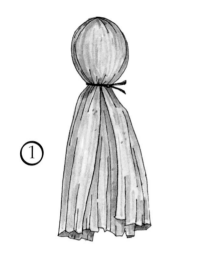
①

Corn had many uses in pioneer times. It was eaten by the pioneers and fed to the livestock. The husks were braided into rugs, baskets, and chair seats, but there were always plenty left over for making dolls. Few pioneer children had store-bought dolls, but any child could make his or her own cornhusk doll.

You need:
- 10 cornhusks
- small Styrofoam® ball
- thread or string
- pipe cleaners

②

1. Gather three cornhusks into a bundle and tie them at one end. To make the head, put the ball under the tied end and pull down the husks to cover it. With a piece of string, tie the husks underneath the ball to make the neck.
2. For the arm piece, wrap a husk around a pipe cleaner and tie it tightly at each end.
3. Tie a piece of husk measuring 3 x 4 inches (7.5 x 10 cm) to the arm piece, about an inch (2.5 cm) from one of the ends. Pull back the husk to make a puffy sleeve and tie it to the arm. Repeat at the other end to make the second sleeve.
4. To make the waist, first center the head between the sleeves. Then tie the husks below the arms.
5. Turn the doll upside-down and place four husks around the waist. Let the wide ends hang over the head. Tie the husks around the waist and then pull down the skirt.
6. To make a male doll, divide the skirt husks into two even sections. Tie each one at the ankle.

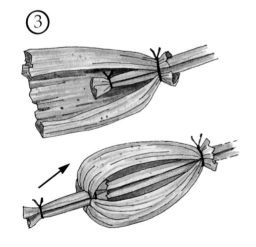
③

④

⑤

⑥

Hints for handling husks:
- you can use husks left over from dinner or bought from a craft store
- cut off sharp tips and stems before using husks
- dry the fresh husks between paper for a few days
- soak the husks in warm water for 15 minutes before using them, so they become soft
- wipe the husks with a towel so they are damp but not wet; a doll made with wet husks will crack and fall apart later

Nature's gifts

To celebrate the seasons, the pioneers decorated their homes with things they found in forests, meadows, or gardens. Pioneers especially celebrated the autumn, which brought the harvest and an end to the year's field work. You, too, can celebrate the seasons by pressing flowers, making wreaths, and creating other decorations with whatever materials nature provides.

Wreath

You need:
- natural objects such as leaves, acorns, pine cones, seed pods, dried flowers and herbs, holly, evergreens, or mistletoe
- grape-vine wreath, which can be bought at a craft shop
- white craft-and-fabric glue
- thin wire
- ribbon or raffia

1. Arrange the natural objects on the wreath.
2. When you are satisfied with how the wreath looks, glue or wire the pieces onto it. Ask for an adult's help.
3. When everything is fastened, let the wreath dry overnight.
4. Tie a bow using the ribbon or raffia and glue or wire it onto your wreath.

Dried-flower frame

You need:
- wooden picture frame
- dried flowers, herbs, berries, orange peels, cinnamon sticks
- white craft-and-fabric glue

1. On the frame, arrange the flowers, leaves, herbs, and any other items you have.
2. When you like the arrangement, begin gluing the pieces onto the frame.
3. When everything is glued, let the frame dry overnight.

Harvest basket

You need:
- basket or box
- squash, colorful dried corn, small pumpkins, and gourds
- burlap and ribbon

1. Line the basket or box with burlap. Let the corners of the burlap hang over the edges of the container.
2. Arrange the vegetables in the container until you are pleased with how they look.
3. Tie a ribbon around the container or its handle.

A. Go on a nature walk to find things for your wreath.
B. Glue and wire your nature finds onto the wreath.
C. Look at all the gifts you can make!
D. Arrange the vegetables in a creative way.

Preserving flowers

There are two easy ways to preserve flowers—air drying and pressing. Air-dried flowers will not lose their shape, but pressed flowers will be flat. Both methods take about two weeks.

- Air dry flowers by tying them in a bunch and hanging them upside down in a dark, dry place.
- Press flowers by spreading petals and leaves between pieces of paper placed in a book. Put a weight on the book.

Kitchen delights

Pioneers preserved the fruits they grew in the summer so they would have food during the winter. One way to preserve fruits was to make jam and marmalade with them. These preserves also made tasty gifts. Here are two easy recipes that are sure to please. Always make sure an adult is present when you use a knife or the stove.

You need:
- 14 ounce (400 ml) can of pure pumpkin
- ¾ cup (180 ml) white sugar
- 1 lemon and peel, chopped, with the seeds removed
- 1 orange and peel, chopped, with the seeds removed
- 1 cup (250 ml) raisins
- 1 teaspoon (5 ml) ginger spice

Pumpkin marmalade

1. In a saucepan, mix all the ingredients, except the pumpkin.
2. Cook on low heat until the sugar melts. Stir often.
3. Add pumpkin. Simmer for 40-60 minutes, stirring often. Let mixture stand until cool.

Applesauce

You need:
- 5 peeled and cored apples
- ¾ cup (180 ml) water
- 1 teaspoon (5 ml) cinnamon

1. Cut the apples into small pieces.
2. Mix the apples, water, and cinnamon in a large saucepan. Stir the ingredients and bring the sauce to a boil.
3. Reduce to low heat and let the sauce simmer until the apples are soft.
4. Remove the pan from the burner and allow the sauce to cool.

Both the pumpkin marmalade and applesauce can be put into sterilized, decorated jars. See page 31.

Scented ornaments

These scented ornaments smell good enough to eat—but don't eat them! They are meant to make your home smell wonderful. The ornaments are also perfect for hanging on a Christmas tree or decorating a present.

You need:
- ½ cup (125 ml) cinnamon
- ½ cup (125 ml) applesauce
- 1 tablespoon (15 ml) white craft-and-fabric glue
- cloves, rice, mustard seeds
- cookie cutters
- ribbon

1. Mix the applesauce, glue, and cinnamon together until they form a stiff dough. Let it stand for 10 minutes.
2. Knead the dough. Sprinkle some cinnamon onto a board. On the board, roll out the dough to the thickness of a pencil.
3. Use a cookie cutter to cut shapes from the dough. Push cloves, rice, or other decorations into the ornament's surface. At the top of the ornament, poke a hole large enough to fit the ribbon.

4. Set your ornament in a warm place to dry. Drying will take about 24 hours. Remember to turn over the ornament so that its underside dries.
5. Once the dough is dry, you can string a ribbon through the hole and hang your ornament anywhere!

Be careful!

After touching the dough, be sure to wash your hands. Do not touch your eyes! Also be careful not to breathe in the cinnamon powder.

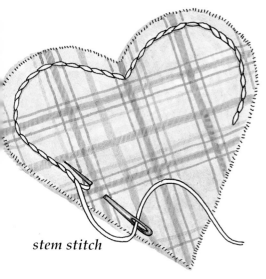

stem stitch

Stitched crafts

Pioneer girls were taught to sew, mend, and embroider at a young age. They sewed scraps of material to make pillow covers, pillows, pot holders, and pin cushions. Sometimes they filled their creations with soft stuffing, and at other times they put sweet-smelling potpourri inside. You can place potpourri hearts in your drawers to make your clothes smell fresh or hang them on the wall to scent the air. If you make a small heart, you can sew buttons on it and wear it as a brooch.

You need:
- scraps of fabric
- scissors
- stuffing
- straight pins
- needle, thread, and yarn
- buttons (optional)
- potpourri (optional)
- safety pin (for the brooch)

Pillow hearts

1. Cut out two same-sized hearts from the fabric. You may want to cut a pattern from paper to use as a cutting guide.
2. Put the hearts together, with the right sides of the fabric facing each other. Pin together the cutouts.
3. Thread a needle and tie a knot at the end of the thread.
4. Using a stem stitch (shown above left), sew small, even stitches around the edge of the heart and leave a small opening. Remove the pins.
5. Turn the heart inside out, so the "right" side of the fabric is on the outside.
6. Fill the heart with stuffing or potpourri.
7. To close the opening, fold the edges of the hole inward. Pin together the opening and neatly stitch it closed. Remove the pins.

A heart brooch

1. Follow step 1 of the pillow hearts, but make your heart cutouts smaller.
2. To decorate your heart, sew buttons onto the right side of the fabric before you stitch together the heart cutouts.
3. Follow steps 2 to 7 of the pillow-heart craft.
4. To make your pillow heart a brooch, stitch a safety pin onto one side.

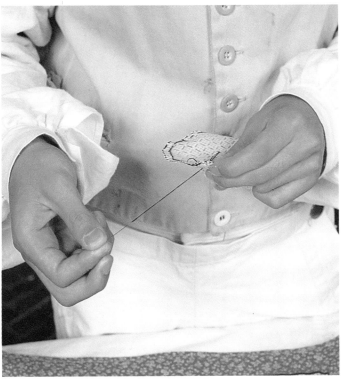

Potpourri pot rest

Pot rests are used to protect table tops from the heat of oven dishes. Potpourri pot rests will also scent a room. When a hot pot or dish is placed on the pot rest, the heat releases the scent of the potpourri. The lovely smell floats through the air and fills the room.

1. Follow steps 1 to 5 on page 14, but use two squares instead of two hearts.
2. Fill the square halfway with stuffing. Put in some potpourri and finish stuffing.
3. To give the pot rest a quilted look, thread pieces of yarn through the pot rest with a needle. Tie the yarn into bows.

Stitched story square

You need:
- paper
- scraps of fabric
- 1 large piece of fabric
- white craft-and-fabric glue
- needle, thread, and yarn
- buttons (optional)

Pioneer women often sewed a story onto each square of a quilt. This type of quilt was given to a bride-to-be or passed down from mothers to daughters. You can make a pillow cover with one story square, or make a quilt by putting together a series of sewn pictures.

1. Draw a scene on a piece of paper or find a picture to use as a guide.
2. From scraps of fabric, cut out the shapes that make up the scene.
3. Arrange the shapes on the large piece of fabric.
4. Put a small dot of glue in the center of each fabric shape and stick them onto the background fabric.
5. Use a running stitch (see below) to sew around the edges of each fabric shape.
6. Add buttons, yarn, or cutouts of trees or people. Create your own design—it is your work of art!

running stitch

Fun with buttons

Before zippers were used in clothing, and long before the invention of Velcro®, clothing was fastened with buttons. After a garment wore out, the life of a button continued. Pioneers found many uses for buttons and were careful to cut them off old clothing. Buttons were used as game pieces, toy parts, decorations, and jewelry.

Button box

You need:
- box with lid
- 2 colors of acrylic paint
- paintbrush and sponge
- white craft-and-fabric glue
- lots of different buttons
- ribbon

1. Using one color, paint the box and its lid. Allow the paint to dry.
2. With a small piece of sponge, dab the second color of paint onto the box. Allow the paint to dry.
3. Glue the buttons onto the box lid.
4. Glue ribbon around the edge of the lid.

Button frame

You need:
- wooden frame
- acrylic paint
- water
- paintbrush
- white craft-and-fabric glue
- lots of different buttons

1. Add water to the acrylic paint to create a thin wash. Paint the frame with it.
2. When the first coat is dry, add a second coat, if needed. Allow it to dry.
3. Select buttons and glue them onto the frame. Before framing a picture, be sure the glue is completely dry and the buttons are securely in place.
4. Ask an adult to help you insert the glass, picture, and frame backing.

A. *You can decorate your heart brooch, described on page 14, with colorful buttons.*
B. *Make a jewelry box or button box and decorate the lid with—what else—buttons!*
C. *Buttons make a plain picture frame look fancy. This one is not yet finished. You can put buttons all the way around the frame.*

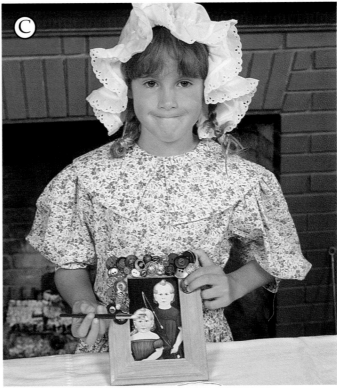

A whizzing whirligig

Pioneer children played with simple toys made from objects found around the home. A large, two-holed button and some string makes a whirligig that spins and hums as long as you can keep it going.

1. Thread the string through the button holes and tie the ends to make a loop. The loop should be as long as your shoulders are wide.
2. Hold the ends of the loop so that the button hangs between your hands. Swing the button around in one direction to wind up the string.
3. Once the string is wound up, quickly pull both ends of the loop outward at the same time. Move your hands together and apart. The button will keep spinning and humming!

The fantastic Jacob's Ladder

The Jacob's Ladder toy was named after a Bible story in which a man named Jacob had a dream. In his dream, he saw a ladder that stretched between heaven and earth. Angels were climbing up and down it. Jacob learned that his descendants would inherit the land on which the ladder stood. The top block of a Jacob's Ladder toy seems to tumble down over the blocks beneath it—resembling someone climbing down a ladder.

Turn the page and learn how to make your own Jacob's Ladder!

Making a Jacob's Ladder

Making a Jacob's Ladder is fun, but playing with it is the best part. You can perform many tricks and make all kinds of shapes with the blocks. Try some of the amazing tricks shown on page 23 with your own Jacob's Ladder. You will have hours of pleasure performing these incredible feats! Impress your parents and dazzle your friends!

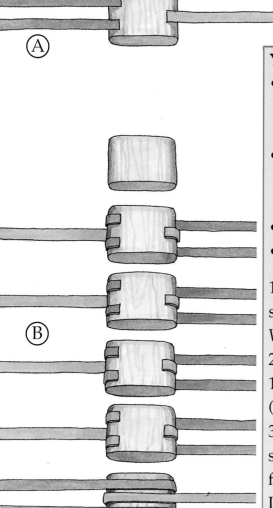

(A)

(B)

(C)

You need:
- 6 plywood squares, ¼ inch (0.5 cm) thick and 2⅛ inches (5.5 cm) square
- a bit more than 9 feet (2.8 m) of ribbon about ¼ inch (0.5 cm) wide
- scissors
- wood glue

1. Make sure the wooden squares are sanded smooth. Watch out for splinters!
2. Cut the ribbon into 15 strips, 5½ inches (14 cm) long.
3. Glue the ribbons, as shown in picture (A), to five of the squares. Leave one square plain. When the glue is dry, fold the ribbons underneath, and arrange the squares as shown in picture (B). Turn one of the squares upside-down (C).
4. Place a square on top of the upside-down square (D). Trim the ribbon of the bottom square and glue it to the top one.
5. When the glue is dry, wrap the ribbon over the top square (E). Place another square on the top and repeat step 4.
6. Repeat steps 4 and 5 until all the squares have been attached with the ribbon (F). The plain square is the last one to be attached.

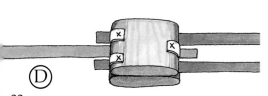

(D)

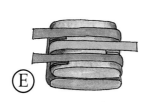

(E)

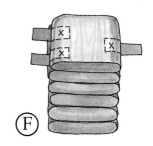

(F)

22

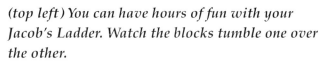

(top left) You can have hours of fun with your Jacob's Ladder. Watch the blocks tumble one over the other.
(bottom left) Make a star or flower!
(top right) Allison has made a butterfly with flapping wings.
(bottom right) This house would become a table if Krista pulled apart the top blocks.

Block and sponge printing

Prints are made by putting paint on a stamp and then pressing the stamp onto a flat surface such as paper, wood, or fabric. The pioneers used plants to make their dyes and paints. Onion skins can be used to make a dark yellow, and berries make red. Today, you can buy paint, but to do this activity pioneer-style, make your own stamps with potatoes, leaves, or sponge pieces.

You need:
- 2 or 3 potatoes
- non-toxic, water-based paints
- wide paintbrush
- newspaper to cover the table
- paring knife
- water
- cutting board
- paper towels or a damp rag
- leaves or sponge pieces
- paper
- jar or glass for water

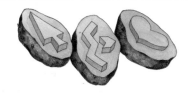

Potato block prints

1. Decide what shapes you want to create.
2. On the cutting board, cut a potato in half. Draw a shape on the flat side of one half. Cut away the potato around your shape so that the design becomes raised.
3. Dip your stamp into paint and press the shape onto paper to make a print.
4. If you want to change the color of your print, wipe the potato and dip it into another color.

Leaf and sponge prints

Brush paint onto a leaf and press it onto paper. To make a sponge stamp, use scissors to cut a shape from a piece of sponge that has a flat side. Dip the stamp into paint and press it onto paper or wood.

Paper projects

To make gift wrap, print on a large piece of paper. Stamp the paper many times to create a pattern. To make stationery, print onto blank envelopes and paper.

The checkerboard design on this tray was printed with a square sponge stamp. What else can you decorate with stamps?

Be careful!

Cutting a shape on a potato can be very tricky. Always have an adult help you use a knife. Make sure to cut away from your body and watch your fingers!

Stenciling and embossing

The pioneers did not have many possessions or much money to decorate their home, so they found simple ways to be creative. Stenciling was an inexpensive and easy way to make walls, furniture, and household objects look more attractive. Using a cut-out pattern, the pioneers painted designs that resembled wallpaper, floor tiles, and other things they could not afford. Stencils also were used to emboss designs onto stationery. You can make a stencil by cutting out a design you have drawn on thin cardboard.

Stenciling

You need:
- stencil
- stencil brush
- acrylic or stencil paints
- jar or glass for water
- newspaper
- masking tape

To stencil a design onto any flat surface, spread newspaper onto your work area and follow these directions:

1. Tape the stencil to the surface you want to decorate.
2. Dip your brush into some paint. Stenciling works best if you have only a little bit of paint on the brush.
3. Lightly dab the brush into the cut-out part of the stencil, as shown above left.
4. If you want to stencil with more than one color, thoroughly clean your brush before you switch paints.

Checkerboard

You need:
- unfinished wooden tray
- fine sandpaper
- damp cloth
- paintbrushes (wide and narrow)
- acrylic and stencil paints
- jar or glass for water
- stencil(s) and stencil brush
- paint tray
- sponge
- scissors
- ruler
- pencil
- 24 wooden shapes for checker pieces (you also can use spools, stones, or other small objects as pieces)

To make a checkerboard, you can use both sponge printing and stenciling.
1. Smooth rough areas on the tray by lightly rubbing them with sandpaper. Wipe the tray with a damp cloth to remove any sawdust or dirt.

2. Paint the tray using acrylic paint and a wide brush. Let the paint dry. Apply a second coat.

3. With a ruler, measure eight equal squares across and eight equal squares down, marking them with a pencil. Using these marks, draw a grid for your checkerboard on the center of the tray.

4. Cut out a sponge square the same size as one checkerboard square.

5. To block print the checkerboard pattern, choose a color of acrylic paint that is different than the color of the tray. Dip the sponge into the paint. Press it onto the first space of the checkerboard grid.

6. Continue the pattern by pressing the sponge stamp onto alternate squares until the checkerboard grid is complete.

7. Let the checkerboard dry overnight.

8. To put a design on the end of the board, follow the stenciling directions on page 26. Let the paint dry and then remove the stencil. Now stencil a design on the opposite end of the tray.

9. Divide the wooden pieces into two piles of twelve. Using one color, paint the pieces in the first pile. Use a different color to paint the other pieces. Set them aside to dry. Decorate the pieces by stenciling on their tops.

Embossed cards

You need:
- heavy craft paper
- stencil
- embossing tool, such as a crochet hook or knitting needle
- masking tape

1. Tape your stencil to a window.

2. Fold the paper in half to form a card.

3. Open the card and place the front, face down, over the stencil.

4. Using the embossing tool, press down on the edge of the stencil. Follow along the entire edge of the cutout.

5. When finished, you will have a raised design on the front of the card.

Decorating with scraps

The art of using paper cutouts to decorate furniture, boxes, trays, and other items is called **decoupage**. It was used in the mid-1800s to add color to items around the home. Scraps, or cutouts, from catalogs and greeting cards were collected and recycled to create beautiful pieces of art.

In the picture above, many small cutouts have been pasted one on top of another. On the opposite page, the children have used fewer cutouts to create their decoupage works of art.

Decoupage still is a good way to recycle greeting cards, magazines, catalogs, wrapping paper, cloth, and leftover wallpaper. You can use decoupage to decorate old boxes, trays, diaries, or furniture. Be sure that the surface you want to cover is clean, dry, and smooth.

Decoupage box

You need:
- wooden or cardboard box
- acrylic paint
- paintbrush
- scraps
- white glue
- water-soluble varnish
- fine sandpaper

1. Paint the box and let it dry overnight.
2. Glue the scraps to the box. You can either apply the glue to the box or the back of the scraps. Continue gluing scraps onto the wood. You may want to glue two or three pieces or overlap many pieces, as shown in the pictures.
3. Gently press out any wrinkles or air bubbles that are trapped beneath the scraps. Allow the scraps to dry for several hours.
4. Brush a thin coat of glue over the pictures and allow it to dry overnight.
5. Apply several coats of varnish, allowing each coat to dry before adding the next one.
6. Lightly sand any bubbles in the varnish.
7. Apply another coat of varnish and allow your creation to dry overnight.

Be careful!

Do not use any varnish without adult supervision! Make sure you work near an open window and do not breathe in any fumes.

Gift-wrapping your crafts

You can use anything you find in your house or yard to make your gifts more attractive. Use your imagination and have fun!

If you want to give some of your crafts as gifts, you can wrap them in a special way. Look around your home for empty jars, boxes, and small baskets. Collect bits of cloth, paper, ribbon, buttons, dried flowers, and leaves to put on top of the presents. You can use glue, tape, a needle and thread, or string and ribbon to attach these ornaments to the gifts. You also can use acrylic paints and sponge or potato stamps to decorate the wrapping paper.

Many of the crafts described in this book can be used to create beautiful wraps! Look at the pictures on these two pages for some more ideas.

Presenting your kitchen crafts

Once you have prepared the marmalade and applesauce described on page 12, you will need something in which to store them. The pioneers preserved many of their foods in jars. Today people still preserve foods, but they also store them in a refrigerator. You can recycle and decorate jars for storing your foods.

You need:
- thoroughly washed and sterilized glass jars with lids
- fabric
- ribbon or string
- white glue
- scissors

1. Use a spoon to scoop your marmalade or applesauce into the jar. When the jar is full, tightly screw on the lid.
2. Cut out a strip of fabric that is large enough to fit around the jar. Glue the strip to the jar.
3. Glue cutouts of cloth or paper to the strip of fabric around the jar.
4. Glue another piece of fabric to the lid or tie a piece of string or ribbon around the fabric to hold it on the lid.

5. You can use bits of ribbon, string, fabric, or even dried fruit peelings to decorate the top of the jar. Attach these items to the lid with glue.

Cloth-wrapped gift

You need:
- 1 piece of fabric large enough to cover the gift
- straight pins
- needle
- yarn or thread
- buttons

1. Center your gift, face down, on the fabric.
2. Fold the sides of the fabric over the present. Pin together the fabric.
3. Thread the needle and tie a knot at the end of the thread or yarn.
4. Stitch together the edges of the fabric. Your sewing does not have to look neat. The important thing is to contain your gift.
5. To finish the present, make a decorative ribbon with buttons and yarn. Thread the buttons onto the yarn and wrap it around the box. Position the buttons on the front of the present.

You can cover the marmalade jar lid with a piece of fabric or slices of dried orange. The applesauce jar can be decorated with dried apple slices and a cinnamon stick. Make sure you keep your jars of preserves in the refrigerator!

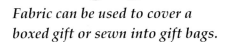

Fabric can be used to cover a boxed gift or sewn into gift bags.

Glossary

Bible A book containing sacred writings of the Jewish and Christian religions

brooch A decorative pin that has a clasp and is worn at the neck or chest

burlap A coarse cloth that is woven from the fiber of the jute plant

cornhusk The leaves covering an ear of corn

decoupage The process of covering a surface with paper or fabric cutouts

descendant Someone who is an offspring of another person

dye A coloring agent that is used to color fabrics, skins, hair, or food

embossing The process of creating a raised design on a surface such as paper

knead To mix ingredients by pressing and squeezing them with one's hands

livestock Farm animals such as cattle, sheep, horses, and pigs

ornament A small decorative object

pioneer A person who is among the first to explore or settle in an area

potpourri A mixture of dried flowers, fruits, herbs, and spices that is used for fragrance

pot rest A padded or braided cloth object on which hot dishes are placed to protect a table or other surface

preserve To prepare food for the purpose of keeping it from spoiling

quilt A bed covering made of three layers that are held together by tiny stitches, which form a pattern such as hearts and circles

raffia A fiber made from leaves of the palm tree

recycling The process of making used objects or materials into new products

stenciling The process of creating a design on a surface, such as a floor or wall, by painting within the cut-out portions of a pattern

sterilize To remove dirt and bacteria

Index

2 3 4 5 6 7 8 9 0   Printed in the U.S.A.   6 5 4 3 2 1 0 9 8 7